Chapter 8

Weather Patterns

You Will Discover

- what causes air currents.
- what kinds of bodies of air make up weather.
- how severe weather forms.
- how weather forecasts are made.
- how climate is different from weather.

Discovery Channel School
Student DVD

online
Student Edition
sfsuccessnet.com

Why does the weather change?

climate

convection current

air mass

Chapter 8 Vocabulary

anemometer

rain gauge

front

barometer

227

Explore How does pressure affect an object?

Materials

marshmallow and marker

plastic jar

straw and clay

metric ruler

plastic mirror

What to Do

1 Draw a target on the marshmallow. Put the marshmallow in the jar.

2 Seal a straw in clay about 2 cm from one of its ends.

3 Put the short end of the straw into the jar. Seal the mouth of the jar with clay.

4 Use a mirror to **observe** the target on the marshmallow. Suck hard on the straw and then blow hard. Quickly repeat 5 times. Observe the target carefully for any small changes in size.

When you blow into the straw, you increase the pressure inside the jar. How can you decrease the pressure?

Process Skills

You used your **observations** of changes in the marshmallow to make an **inference.**

Explain Your Results

1. How did the marshmallow change when the pressure was increased and decreased?

2. **Infer** Why did the size of the marshmallow change when the pressure increased?

Reading Skills

Draw Conclusions

Learning to **draw conclusions** can help you evaluate what you read and **observe.**

- As you read, put together facts and then extend them to form a conclusion or to make an **inference.**

- Sometimes you may have more than one conclusion.

- You might change your conclusions when you get more facts.

Science Article

Rising to the Heights

Soon after people started flying in hot-air balloons, they began measuring air conditions above Earth's surface. Researchers who wanted to understand weather rose high into the air. But these flights were dangerous. At higher altitudes, air pressure can be dangerously low. In 1862, a pair of researchers rose so high they barely survived their flight. One passed out due to a lack of oxygen at the high altitude. The other could barely move for the same reason. He used his teeth to operate the balloon's controls and bring it down.

Apply It!

Make a graphic organizer like this one. List facts from the science article and **draw a conclusion.**

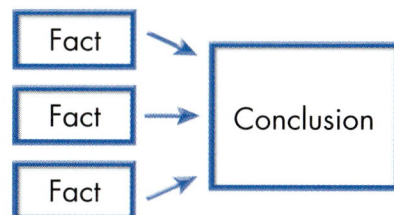

Fact	→	
Fact	→	Conclusion
Fact	→	

🔊 You Are There!

A cold wind blows around you as you climb higher up the ice-covered mountain. You spend a moment adjusting the tank on your back. At this altitude, you need a tank of oxygen to help you breathe. As you look at the clouds below, you think about all the planning that went into your climb. You are especially thankful that the weather forecasters could tell that this would be a good week for climbing. How were they able to predict this good weather?

AudioText 🔊

How does air move?

Air is a mixture of gases in constant motion. Differences in air temperatures create winds.

Layers of Air

Take a very deep breath. You now probably have about 3 liters of air in your lungs. The air has many gases in it. About $\frac{8}{10}$ of the air is nitrogen and about $\frac{2}{10}$ is oxygen. A very small part of the air is carbon dioxide, water vapor, and other gases. No other planet in the Solar System has air that is like Earth's.

There are five layers of Earth's atmosphere. Most weather conditions happen only in the bottom layer, the troposphere. As you go up through the five layers, temperatures and air pressure change. Air pressure decreases as you go up through the atmosphere. This decrease happens because the gas particles in the air get farther apart and there is less air above you.

1. **✔Checkpoint** As altitude increases, how does air pressure change? Why?

2. **Writing in Science** **Narrative** In your **science journal,** describe the layers and gases of Earth's atmosphere. Write as if you were a space traveler from another planet approaching Earth and making a report to your headquarters.

Exosphere

Thermosphere

Altitude: about 600 km Temperature: 1700°C

Mesosphere

Altitude: about 85 km Temperature: −90°C

Stratosphere

Altitude: about 50 km Temperature: 0°C

Altitude: about 8–15 km Temperature: −55°C

Troposphere

Convection Currents

Have you ever walked over hot sand to get to the cool water of a lake or ocean? Land gets warm more quickly in sunlight than does water. At night, land cools faster than water. This causes the air above the land and water to have different temperatures. Differences in the temperatures of air result in winds, storms, and all sorts of weather.

Different temperatures also cause convection currents to form. In a **convection current**, gases or liquids rise and sink in a circular path.

In cool air, gas particles are closer together than in warm air. This means that every liter of cool air is heavier than every liter of warm air. When the two kinds of air are next to each other, the cool air will sink and force the warm air to rise.

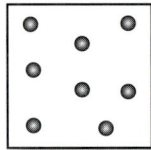

cool air   **warm air**

The kind of convection current shown here occurs near oceans and very large lakes during the daytime. Another convection current will flow in the opposite direction at night. These currents can form daily patterns of clouds, rain, wind, and air pressure.

Rising air will cool. It stops rising when it is the same temperature as surrounding air. This cooled air is pushed over the water by the rising air below it.

The cool water will not warm the air above it as much as the land warms the air above it. So, the cool air sinks below the warm air.

Cool, sinking air causes high air pressure at the surface.

As the cool air moves under the warm air, wind is created. Wind occurs as air moves from a place of high air pressure to a place of low air pressure.

Six huge convection currents form in the air above Earth. Part of the reason for these currents is that tropical regions get warmer than other parts of Earth. Warm air from tropical regions rises. After the air cools, it sinks farther north and south.

The combination of the movement of the huge convection currents and the spinning of Earth cause regional surface wind patterns. Winds generally blow from west to east over much of the United States.

Jet streams are found high above the ground between these huge convection currents. A jet stream is a band of very fast wind formed by the different temperatures between the convection currents. Even though it is very high, a jet stream can change temperature, winds, and precipitation by affecting the movement of air.

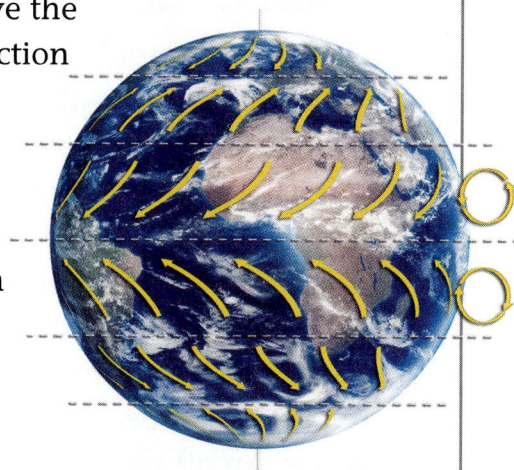

Six huge convection currents around Earth result in regional surface wind patterns.

Warm, rising air causes a low air pressure at the surface

The warm land makes air above it warm. This warm air is forced up by the cool air, causing sea breezes.

✓ **Lesson Checkpoint**

1. What causes convection currents?
2. In what direction do surface winds over the United States generally blow?
3. **Draw Conclusions** At night, land cools more than water. Air above land will be cooler than air above the water. What conclusion can you draw about convection currents near the ocean at night?

What are air masses?

There are four basic bodies of air. These large bodies of air drift across the globe. When they are pushed together, the weather can change.

Kinds of Air Masses

Suppose your cousins just returned from a trip. You want to figure out where they went. When they show you the seashells they collected, you know that your cousins were at a beach. You can figure out where air has been too. The air's temperature and water vapor content can give you clues.

If air stays over an area for some time, it takes on properties of that area and becomes an air mass. An **air mass** is a large body of air with similar properties all through it. The most important properties are temperature and amount of water vapor. An air mass keeps its original properties for a while as it moves to a new area.

Four kinds of air masses are seen in the picture to the right. Generally, the kind of weather you have at any time is because of the air mass in your area. If you are having several warm, clear days, the weather will remain that way until a new air mass comes into your area. Some kinds of weather usually happen only at the edges of air masses.

Air masses move because of winds. These winds may be near the ground. Some air masses are guided by the jet stream high above the ground. If the jet stream guides an air mass from Canada to the middle of the United States, northerly winds will probably bring cold, dry air. At the edge of this air mass, storms may occur.

1. ✔**Checkpoint** How do air masses form and move?
2. **Writing in Science** **Descriptive** In a letter, a friend wonders why the weather has been so hot and humid. In your **science journal,** write a reply to your friend explaining the role of air masses in making the weather hot and humid.

Continental Polar Air
The land near the poles is
not very moist. So, the air
mass from this area is cold
and fairly dry.

Maritime Tropical Air
Humid air has lots of moisture.
Over tropical oceans or
rainforests, an air mass
becomes warm and very
humid because water can
easily evaporate there.

Maritime Polar Air
Even though the ocean near
the poles is cold, water vapor
evaporates into the air. An air
mass forming over the poles is
cold and moist.

Continental Tropical Air
A large hot desert can cause
the air above it to be warm
and fairly dry.

When Air Masses Meet

Have you ever seen a line of clouds move from the horizon until it is overhead? What you have probably seen is the arrival of a front. A **front** is a boundary between two air masses. Most air masses move from west to east over the United States, so fronts have the same motion.

A front gets its name from the kind of air that moves into the area. A cold front brings colder air into an area. A warm front brings warmer air into an area. Sometimes a front does not move very much or it moves back and forth over the same area. This kind of front is called a stationary front.

Notice in the pictures shown that both fronts have rising warm air. Areas of rising air near the fronts have lower air pressure than areas in the middle of the air masses. Rising air at fronts often causes rain or snow.

When cooler air moves in, it forces warmer air to move up quickly. The rising air forms cumulus clouds along the steep boundary. Heavy precipitation often falls at a cold front.

Cold Front

Cold air

Warm air

Notice that near this steep cold front, people on the ground might see a line of clouds over them just before the cooler air arrives. Have you ever felt the temperature drop quickly as clouds move into your area?

At warm fronts, warmer air moves against cooler air. The warmer air gradually rises above the cooler air. The clouds of a warm front often move more slowly and cause longer periods of precipitation than cold fronts.

Warm Front

Cold air

Warm air

Notice that near a warm front, people on the ground might see high-altitude clouds form above them long before they feel the warmer air arrive at ground level.

✔**Lesson Checkpoint**

1. Why does precipitation often happen at fronts?

2. Suppose one morning, you need a light coat to play outside. A thunderstorm forces you to go inside for several hours. That afternoon, you need a heavy coat to go outside. What kind of front has passed?

3. 🎯 **Draw Conclusions** An air mass moves into the middle of the United States. It has low humidity and high temperatures. Where can you conclude that this air mass formed?

What causes severe weather?

Sometimes the water cycle can lead to severe weather. Severe weather includes thunderstorms, tornadoes, and hurricanes.

Thunderstorms

What kind of severe weather happens in your part of the country? Do you have thunderstorms, tornadoes, hurricanes, or blizzards? Just having very high or low temperatures can be dangerous. If you know that severe weather is coming, you need to prepare for it.

Thunderstorms can form in different ways. Often, the first stage of a thunderstorm has strong, quickly rising currents of moist air. Clouds grow as moisture condenses in the rising air. The clouds have both ice crystals and water droplets.

In the storm's second stage, precipitation starts to fall, which pulls some air down with it. The storm now has both upward and downward moving currents.

In the storm's final stage, all the currents are moving downward, and the clouds get smaller as precipitation falls. Remember that the condensation and precipitation of thunderstorms are parts of the water cycle.

1. **✓Checkpoint** List four examples of severe weather.
2. **Draw Conclusions** Why do you think you should get inside as soon as possible when there is a severe storm warning?

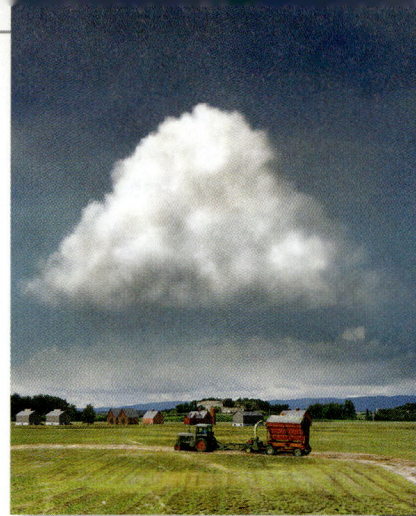

First stage: All air currents move upward.

Second stage: Air currents are mixed.

Final stage: All air currents move downward.

Different areas of a thunderstorm cloud have either positive or negative electrical charges. This may be caused by the precipitation colliding in the air currents of the cloud.

Lightning is a large electrical spark moving between areas of opposite charge. Lightning can warm air to 30,000°C in a fraction of a second. This high temperature causes the air to expand so rapidly that it makes vibrations in the air. We hear these vibrations as thunder.

What we see as one flash of lightning is often many flashes of both positive and negative charges going up and down.

Lightning often hits tall objects. If you cannot get inside a building during a thunderstorm, move away from trees or high towers. Stay low but do not lie on the ground.

The negative charges on the cloud cause positive charges to gather in the ground below.

Watches and Warnings

A **severe thunderstorm watch** means that severe thunderstorms with high winds and hail might form.

A **severe thunderstorm warning** means that severe thunderstorms have formed and you should prepare for them. Get inside as soon as possible.

Tornadoes

Many things happen as a tornado forms. Layers of wind in a storm blow at different speeds or in different directions. Between these layers, a column of air starts spinning like a log rolling on its side. Then, upward winds lift one end of this spinning column. Downward winds push down on the other end. This spinning column of air is called a funnel cloud. It is called a tornado if it touches the ground.

Tornadoes usually last only a few minutes, but they can leave a path many kilometers long and hundreds of meters wide. Winds in a tornado move at hundreds of kilometers per hour. These winds can move cars and buildings around with ease.

If you hear or see a tornado warning, take shelter right away. It is best to go into a basement. If you cannot, go to a closet or windowless room in the center of the building. Why do you think it is important to stay away from windows?

West wind

South wind

Air rolls between two layers of winds.

The rolling air is turned so it stands upright and becomes a funnel cloud. It is a tornado if it touches the ground.

Hurricanes

Hurricanes get their energy from warm ocean water. When water vapor from the ocean condenses, it releases energy. Under the right conditions, this energy builds and drives the winds of a hurricane. Once it is over land, the hurricane's energy is reduced.

Even though the swirling winds of a hurricane are not as fast as a tornado's winds, the winds of these ocean storms are more destructive. Why?

First, hurricanes last for days, possibly hitting several locations. Second, a hurricane is hundreds of kilometers wide. Third, hurricanes can result in huge waves that cause severe damage and flood the shore. Heavy rains can also cause floods in areas farther inland.

Hurricane as seen from above.

Preparing for Hurricanes

To prepare for a hurricane, board up your windows. Store food and water. Have flashlights and battery-powered radios available. Put valuables in plastic containers high off the ground. Most importantly, stay inside. If authorities call for an evacuation, leave immediately. Why do you think these actions are helpful?

✓ Lesson Checkpoint

1. What is the cause of a tornado?
2. What are the effects of a hurricane?
3. **Writing in Science** **Persuasive** Prepare a poster, play, or radio advertisement that would persuade people that severe weather is dangerous and tells what they can do to be safe.

241

How are weather forecasts made?

People use many kinds of instruments to collect weather data. Weather forecasts are based on the data collected.

Collecting Data

What exactly is weather? How would you define it? To completely describe a weather system at any particular place and time, you need to describe all its parts: the temperature, moisture, clouds, precipitation, wind speed, air pressure, and wind direction. All of these parts may interact with each other and change during the course of a day. They may change even more quickly than that!

Many kinds of tools measure all these parts of the weather. Some of these instruments might even be in your home. What weather-measuring tool have you used that is not shown here?

A **barometer** shows air pressure. In some barometers, air pressure pushes mercury up a tube. The barometer shown here has a small sealed container connected to the dial. When air pressure squeezes on the container, it causes the dial of the barometer to move.

An **anemometer** measures wind speed. The wind makes the cups of the anemometer spin around. Cups spin faster as winds move faster.

A hygrometer measures the moisture in the air. Some hygrometers have a pointer attached to horsehair. The hair shortens in drier air, moving the pointer.

Horsehair hygrometer

Weather Records				
	Lowest Average Yearly Rainfall	Highest Average Yearly Rainfall	Highest Temperature	Lowest Temperature
USA	4.00 cm	1,168 cm	57°C	–62°C
World	0.08 cm	1,168 cm	58°C	–89°C

Anemometer

Rain gauge

A **rain gauge** measures how much rain has fallen. The top of the rain gauge may be wider than the bottom. This allows the rain gauge to catch more rain when a small amount falls. It also makes measuring small amounts of rain easier.

Radar can measure the winds and precipitation inside a storm. The radar station sends out energy similar to signals from a radio station. Some of the energy bounces back from objects, including raindrops. Changes in the returning energy show the direction and speed of a rainstorm.

1. ✓**Checkpoint** What are the parts of a weather system?
2. **Writing in Science** **Descriptive** Write in your **science journal** a description of daily and seasonal weather changes in your area.

Doppler radar tower

Computerized weather stations collect and report many kinds of data.

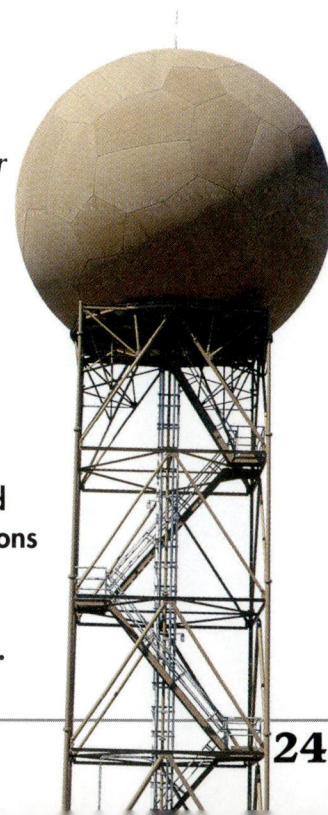

Weather Forecasts

Have you noticed any daily or seasonal patterns of change in the weather? For example, temperatures have a pattern of rising and falling during each day. Another pattern of temperature changes occurs throughout the seasons of the year. Temperatures rise and fall from January to December. There are also seasonal patterns of precipitation. Spring often has lots of precipitation.

Weather forecasters observe many patterns of weather change. They use the information from their observations to make inferences. These inferences are conclusions of how air, land, and the steps of the water cycle affect each other to make weather systems. With these inferences, forecasters make predictions, saying what the weather most likely will be in the future.

Forecasters make their predictions by assuming that current weather will behave like similar weather in the past. The more similar the conditions are, the more likely they will develop in the same way. The more information forecasters have when making this comparison, the better their predictions will be.

Forecasters use weather maps to display current weather conditions and their predictions. There are many kinds of weather maps, but most follow the same general rules. Look at the weather map on page 245. The key next to the weather map tells what the symbols and colors mean.

By themselves, the lines for fronts can tell you much about the current weather. First, the triangles or half-circles on the lines point in the direction the front is moving. Warm fronts bring warmer weather. Cold fronts bring cooler weather. Remember that fronts are always in places of low pressure. In most of the United States, fronts generally move from west to east. They often bring cloudy weather, but areas of high pressure that are away from fronts often have clear skies.

The first weather satellite was launched in 1960.

1940

The first kind of weather balloon carried instruments in 1927.

1910

1900

1890

1880

1870

1860

The telegraph was invented in 1844. It was soon used to transmit weather reports.

1830

Temperature Key

–7°C	–1°C	4°C	10°C	16°C	21°C	27°C	32°C	

✓Lesson Checkpoint

1. Read the weather map. What was the weather like in your part of the country when this map was made?

2. What kind of weather system is found in areas of high air pressure? low air pressure?

3. **Technology** in Science For three days, use government Web sites to track data from weather maps, weather satellites, radar, barometers, thermometers, and anemometers. Use the patterns in your data to make a display describing what you think the weather will be like on the fourth day.

Common Weather Symbols

Symbol	Meaning
H	Area of high air pressure
L	Area of low air pressure
	Warm front
	Cold front
	Stationary front
	Snow
	Rain
	Thunderstorms
	Sunny
	Cloudy
	Partly cloudy

What is climate?

Weather and climate are not the same thing. The climate of an area does not change as often as the weather.

Weather and Climate

The words *weather* and *climate* do not have the same definitions. Weather is made up of all the conditions in one place at a single moment. Weather changes very often. **Climate** is the average of weather conditions over a long time, usually thirty years. Climate includes things like the average amount of precipitation, the average temperature, and how much the temperature changes during the year. Climates do not change as much as the daily weather does.

Landforms Affect Climate

Mountain ranges may have different climates than areas around them. Higher land is cooler because temperature decreases with height in the troposphere. But that is not the only way that climate varies around mountains.

Areas on opposite sides of a mountain range can have very different climates. For example, the west side of the Cascade Mountains in the western United States has a wet climate. It can get more than 2.5 m of precipitation each year. Temperate rain forests grow on this side of the mountains. But the area east of the mountains has a dry climate, like a desert. This happens because the air does not have much moisture in it by the time it reaches the east side.

As moist winds blow from the ocean, the mountains force the air to rise and cool. This makes clouds. Water condenses in the clouds and falls as rain or snow. This water cycle is shown here.

Oceans Affect Climate

Oceans can affect a climate by slowing the rise and fall of the air temperature. Remember that bodies of water become warm and cool more slowly than land. Because of this, the temperature of the air near an ocean does not change as quickly as air inland. In the winter, ocean beaches often do not get as cold as areas just a few miles inland. In the summer, the air over ocean beaches is often cooler than air over areas inland.

Ocean currents can make a climate warmer or cooler. The Gulf Stream and the North Atlantic Drift are large currents that carry warm water northward. The water warms the winds above it. These winds make northern Europe's climate much warmer than it would be otherwise. A change in these currents could change the climate of Europe. On the other hand, cold currents that flow from Alaska to California make that coastal climate cooler.

1. **✓Checkpoint** How are weather and climate different?
2. **Writing in Science** **Persuasive** Consider how the jet stream, oceans, mountains, and the water cycle affect climate. Write a paragraph in which you try to persuade the reader that one of them has the biggest effect on the climate in your area.

The air becomes drier after the rain or snow has fallen.

Air sinking down the side of a mountain does not make clouds or rain. This area is in a rain shadow.

Past Climates

Climates are determined by many years of weather, but that does not mean that climates do not change. In the 1600s, the climates of North America and Europe were much colder and wetter than they are now. This time is known as the Little Ice Age. Many written records of the weather during this time still exist.

Researchers can find clues about climate changes before written records. For example, during major ice ages huge glaciers moved across continents. They moved soil and rock of every size to form hills and lakes. Researchers can tell how the glaciers moved by making maps of these hills and lakes.

Climates have changed many times throughout history, sometimes quickly, but usually slowly. Looking at fossils is one way that scientists try to learn about climates in times before written records. Scientists assume that if an ancient plant looks very much like a modern plant, the two plants need the same kind of climate. For example, suppose a scientist working in a desert finds a fossil that looks like a fern. Since modern ferns do not survive in deserts, this fossil would be a clue that the area was once more wet than it is today. The same kind of comparison is done with fossils of animals and other organisms.

Fossils of ferns are found in areas that were likely warm and humid in the past.

The white areas on this map are places covered by glaciers during the last Major Ice Age.

Volcano eruptions may have changed climates in the past.

This crater was caused by an impact of a meteorite.

How Climates Change

There are many events that might cool a climate. The Little Ice Age may have occured because the Sun produced less energy. Volcanic eruptions and asteroid or meteorite impacts may have quickly caused cooler climates in the distant past. They could have done this by putting dust and other materials into the upper atmosphere. These materials can cool the climate by blocking sunlight or reflecting sunlight back into space.

Carbon dioxide, methane, and water vapor also can make climates warmer. They can be produced by human activities, such as burning coal and gasoline. These gases can also enter the atmosphere naturally, such as through decaying matter, forest fires, volcanoes, and the water cycle.

Many different events help to form a climate. Because of this, it is hard to determine why a climate has changed. Scientists have had debates on these changes and will probably have more in the future.

✓ Lesson Checkpoint

1. How are fossils used to study past climates?
2. What can cause a sudden climate change?
3. **Math in Science** During the last century, many places became warmer, but some became cooler. From 1901 to 1930, the average temperature for Waco, Texas, was 19.36°C. From 1971 to 2000, the average temperature was 18.57°C. How much did the temperature change?

Investigate How does a thermometer work?

Materials

plastic jar and metric ruler

room-temperature water

red food coloring

plastic straw and clay

bowls of very warm water and very cold water

What to Do

1 Fill the jar 2 cm full with room-temperature water. Add red food coloring until the water turns red.

2 cm

2 Put the straw in the water. Do not let it touch the bottom of the jar.

3 Use clay to seal the mouth of the jar and the straw in place.

You have made a thermometer!

4 Place your thermometer in the very warm water. **Observe** whether the red liquid in the straw moves higher, moves lower, or does not change. Record your observation.

Be careful! Do not use dangerously hot water!

5 **Predict** whether the red liquid in the straw will move higher or lower when you place the thermometer in cold water. Record your prediction. Test your prediction and record your observation.

Thermometer in Warm Water	Thermometer in Cold Water	
Observation	Prediction	Observation

Explain Your Results

1. What evidence did you use to make your **prediction?**

2. Explain how you think your thermometer works.

Go Further

How could you use weather instruments to describe weather patterns and how weather changes? Collect and analyze weather data.

Analyzing Tornado Data

Somewhere in the United States, thunderstorms may produce tornadoes this month. Tornadoes happen during all times of the year, and they happen in every state. The bar graph shows the average number of tornadoes that happen each month in the United States.

Average Number of U.S. Tornadoes Per Month

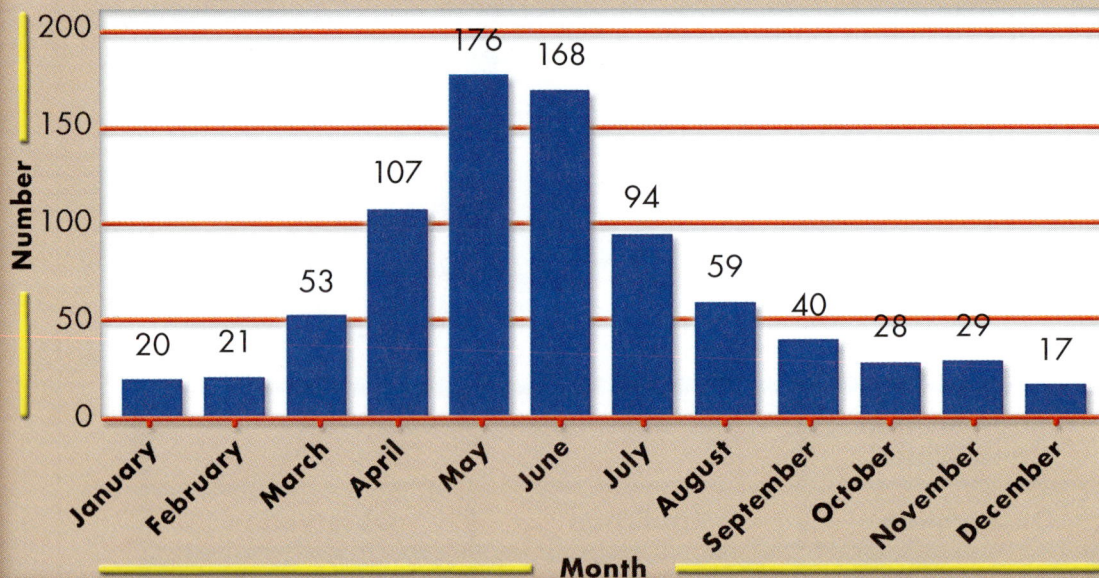

Month	Number
January	20
February	21
March	53
April	107
May	176
June	168
July	94
August	59
September	40
October	28
November	29
December	17

One way to describe a pattern in the data above is to use ranges. Ranges show how much the data changes. A lower range shows less change. A higher range shows more change. For example, the range in the three months of January, February, and March is 53 – 20, or 33. The range in the three months of March, April, and May is 176 – 53, or 123. So, the change in the number of tornadoes each month from March through May is almost four times the change from January through March!

Use the graph to answer the following questions.

1. What is the range from June through August?
   A. 146
   C. 85
   B. 109
   D. 74

2. What is the range in the number of tornadoes from September through February?
   F. 59
   H. 23
   G. 40
   I. 19

3. Between which two months does the number of tornadoes change the most?
   A. March–April
   B. April–May
   C. May–June
   D. June–July

4. Between which two months does the number of tornadoes change the least?
   F. January–February
   G. February–March
   H. March–April
   I. April–May

5. The number of tornadoes from January through May
   A. increases by 109.
   B. decreases by 109.
   C. increases by 156.
   D. decreases by 156.

Lab zone Take-Home Activity

Record the outside air temperature throughout one day in your **science journal.** At what time is the temperature at its highest point? lowest point? Is the greatest change in the morning, afternoon, evening, or overnight?

Use Vocabulary

air mass (p. 234)	**convection current** (p. 232)
anemometer (p. 242)	**front** (p. 236)
barometer (p. 242)	**rain gauge** (p. 243)
climate (p. 246)	

Use the terms from the list above that best completes each sentence.

1. A(n) _____ measures wind speed.

2. A(n) _____ measures air pressure.

3. A(n) _____ measures the amount of rain.

4. A(n) _____ is the average weather conditions over many years.

5. A(n) _____ is a circular current of air.

6. A(n) _____ is a large body of air with generally the same temperature and moisture.

7. A(n) _____ is a boundary between two air masses.

Explain Concepts

8. Explain why the weather changes.

9. How are the water cycle in an area and the climate in the same area related?

10. How do weather forecasters make predictions about tomorrow's weather?

Process Skills

11. **Interpret the Data** The chart compares weather conditions in the same area at noon on two summer days. Interpret the data to conclude what type of front moved through the area.

Day	Noon Temperature
Monday	28°C
Tuesday	20°C

12. **Predict** St. Louis, Missouri, experiences large differences in temperature between summer and winter. Predict how the temperature difference would change if St. Louis were next to an ocean.

13. **Predict** what would happen if the amount of energy Earth gets from the Sun were to slowly decrease over time.

Draw Conclusions

14. Make a graphic organizer like the one shown below. Fill in your conclusion.

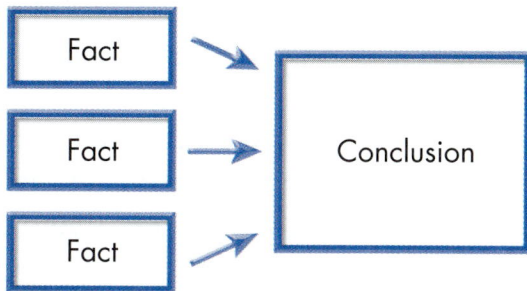

```
[Fact] →
            → [Conclusion]
[Fact] →
[Fact] →
```

Fact: Gas particles become more spread out at higher altitudes.
Fact: At higher altitudes, there is less air above you pushing down so the air pressure is lower.
Fact: Mountain climbers need oxygen tanks to breathe well at high altitudes.

Test Prep

15. Where are clouds most likely to form?
  Ⓐ in a rain shadow
  Ⓑ in rising air
  Ⓒ in sinking air
  Ⓓ in high pressure

16. What causes air currents?
  Ⓕ uneven heating of Earth's surface
  Ⓖ boundaries between air masses
  Ⓗ air heated by lightning
  Ⓘ changes in wind direction

17. What does a capital letter H on a weather map show?
  Ⓐ a hurricane
  Ⓑ hot air
  Ⓒ high pressure
  Ⓓ heavy rain

18. What type of air mass comes from polar ocean areas?
  Ⓕ cold and dry
  Ⓖ cold and moist
  Ⓗ warm and dry
  Ⓘ warm and moist

19. Explain why the answer you selected for Question 18 is best. For each of the answer choices you did not select, give a reason why it is not the best choice.

20. **Writing in Science** **Descriptive**
Write a description of one type of severe weather and explain how it forms. Then describe what can be done to stay safe in that kind of severe weather.

Atmospheric Scientist

Lin Chambers works with other scientists to understand how light energy flows through clouds.

When Lin Chambers was young, she and her family lived in Europe. Almost every year, they flew back to the United States for a visit. Those airplane rides inspired Chambers to study aeronautical engineering in college.

Chambers got her first full-time job at NASA. She studied how spacecraft heat up as they travel through the atmosphere. A few years later, she began to work on a project to study how light energy and heat energy move in and out of Earth's atmosphere. Chambers focuses on how light energy flows through clouds. She compares measurements from satellites with measurements taken from the ground. She runs computer models to understand how clouds can change the direction of light flow through the atmosphere.

Chambers works with many other scientists. Each scientist analyzes data in different ways. The scientists check each other's work and discuss different conclusions they can draw. Working as a team, each scientist is responsible for a different piece of the problem. The project goal is to produce accurate data about Earth's climate. Chambers says, "We rely on each other," stressing the importance of collaboration in her work.

Chambers loves studying clouds. It brings her back to the reason for her first career choice. Thinking about her experience on airplanes she admits, "The thing I enjoyed most about it was sitting at the window, looking down at the clouds."

Lab zone Take-Home Activity

Keep your own cloud journal in your **science journal,** identifying cloud types. Also find out about and look for the clouds known as contrails. Record information about the weather. Write down the date and time of your observations. Draw conclusions about cloud types and the weather, and compare your conclusions with those of a friend.

EC NTL 10 9 8 7 6 5 4 3 2